Proverbs for Kids

and those who love them

Volume 1

How God Teaches
Wisdom Using

things around the house

Robert M. Gullberg

My Proverbs Study Book

Presented to:_____
By:_____
Date:_____

Proverbs for Kids- Proverbs for Kids- Ten Volume Series:

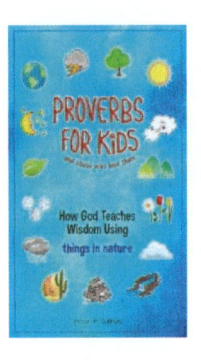

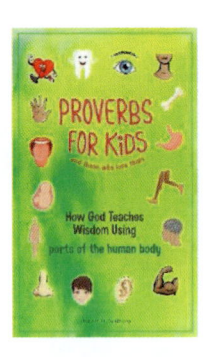

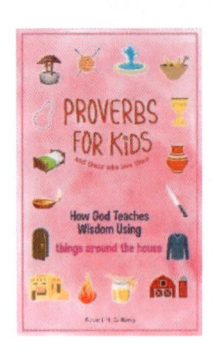

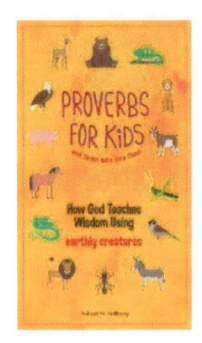

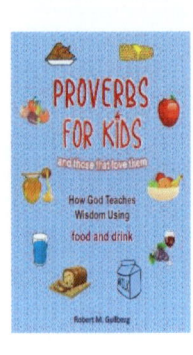

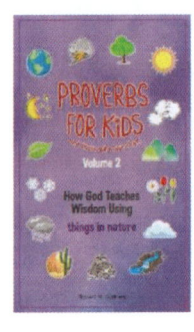

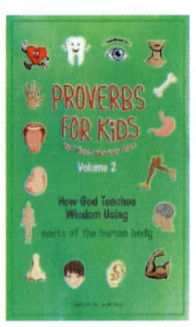

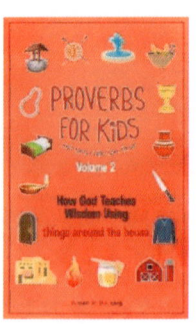

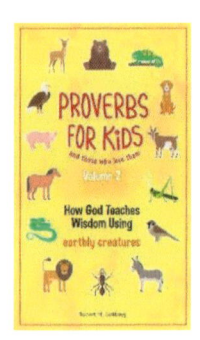

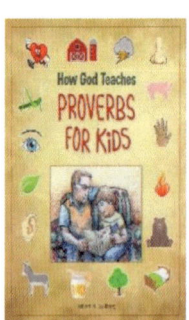

Written by Robert M. Gullberg M.D., E-book or print version available at **amazon.com or christianbooks.now.site**. All rights reserved. No part of this publication may be reproduced in any form without written permission from *In House Faith Publishing* at rgullberg@wi.rr.com

Printed in the United States of America

Acknowledgements: All Scripture verses taken from the *NIV (New International Version) Bible*, *Living Bible*, or *The Message* (Public Domain). All images are free and not copyrighted. Teachable Truths come from numerous internet sources. Cover Art: Shad Smith. Thanks to John R. Gullberg, Laurie Stecher, and Jim Magruder for editorial assistance.

Contents

A Word from the Author……………………………………………………………………….4

Barn- Learn to be *generous* with all that you have, and
God will be honored………………………………………………………………………………**7**

Clothing- Help those who are in need. Be *compassionate*.
Feel for those who are hurting……………………………………………………………**12**

Fire- Do everything without arguing or complaining. *Stay
away from gossip*……………………………………………………………………………….**16**

Lamp- *Treat your parents with honor and respect*. Then your
days on earth will be long…………………………………………………………………..**20**

Ornament- Learn to *accept criticism well* and *be a good
listener*. Read and study the Bible………………………………………………………**24**

Reaping/Sowing- *Work on being good* and God will reward
you for it. *Don't give up*……………………………………………………………………..**28**

Tent- *God says your heart is more important than what kind
of house that you live in. Don't be jealous of others.*……………………………**34**

Well- Learn to *have a pure heart*, and live like
a person who has godly values……………………………………………………………**39**

Following God………………………………………………………………………………….**44**

Proverbs in this Book………………………………………………………………………**45**

Principles Taught in this Book……………………………………………………………**45**

A Word from the Author

Ever wonder how God talks to kids?

God is the greatest storyteller, and throughout the Bible he uses creative and inspiring ways to help us learn Biblical truths. He often uses the "things of this world" such as clouds, the sun, oceans, darkness, deserts, light, the wind, water, earthly creatures, parts of the human body, and everyday things around the house (to name a few!) to teach us eternal truths. In the Old Testament, God teaches us his timeless wisdom from the Book of Proverbs. In the New Testament, Jesus tells numerous stories, called parables, to help teach deep spiritual lessons. He uses common concepts such as farming, money, fig trees, soil, doors, and fishing to teach important life lessons. The practical teachings contained in Proverbs were inspired by God and given to mankind over 2,000 years ago. The book was written around 920 B.C. primarily by King Solomon. According to the Bible, he was the wisest man who has ever lived. While 920 B.C. was a long time ago, his teaching principles still hold true for today!

Proverbs for Kids is a ten-volume series of inspirational books each covering over 90 proverbs designed to teach children Biblical truths in a fun, easy, and entertaining way. These concepts captivate the imagination and help kids understand important truths in a language they can understand. What's more is both kids and adults who read to them will enjoy these informative and colorful books. The books are especially good for kids between 5 and 11 years of age. This volume in the series shows how God uses **things around the house** to help explain foundational spiritual truths. As we look at common things around the house, we see God teach us his wisdom. The other books in this series are about **parts of the human body, earthly creatures, food and drink, and things in nature**.

Each of the books in the series contain **Teachable Truths** and the **Take Home Points** to explain the proverb(s) in more detail. There are **Other Key Verses** from the Bible to reinforce the point of the proverb. Many of these verses of scripture serve as great memory verses and they are contained at the end of each section.

The **Conclusion** at the end of each topic reinforces the *main point* of the Proverb to make memorable teaching. The books in the *Proverbs for Kids* series are easy to navigate with enlarged pictures that accompany the associated Proverbs.

The *Proverbs for Kids* book series coupled with the time you invest reading to your kids or grandchildren will engrain Biblical wisdom they can draw on for the rest of their lives!

With so many difficult challenges we face to raise godly children in today's upside-down culture, it is important to introduce them from a young age to God who loves them dearly. Learning about God together is the right way to go and will enhance our family relationships even more.

As you read through Proverbs for Kids, you will be able to picture yourself growing up in Israel during Bible times to see how God used *things around the house* to teach us his wisdom. That wisdom is the same today as it was yesterday. May God use this book to draw many young hearts and minds toward understanding spiritual truth and right ways of living. I hope this inspirational book will be a great adventure for your family.

-Robert M. Gullberg

If you have a quick moment, it would mean a lot if you could go to your "orders" page on Amazon to leave a review for this book. Thank you.

Comments on the Proverbs for Kids series:

Sullivan Bell, 7 years old, said "I love the drawings and the stories."

Sawyer Bell, 8-1/2 years old, said "I like the books because they teach me about God and his wisdom."

Brooklyn Bell, 11 years old, said "It is a good learning experience for me because I like studying with my grandpa."

Jack Bell (grandpa), *Navigator Representative, professional Life and Leadership Coach, said* "It has been fun teaching God's truth from Proverbs for Kids. It has created a whole new spiritual dimension with me and my grandchildren. It fulfills **Deuteronomy 4:9 and 6:7**--*"God tells us to impress his commandments on our children and their children after them and to talk about them when we sit at home and when we walk along the road, when we lie down and when we get up."*

To review the author's other faith books for children, teens and adults, go to **Christianbooks.now.site** or scan this QR code:

Barn

Barns store things on a farm –such as hay and animals

Teachable Truths:

Barns have been built since farms existed thousands of years ago. In Israel during the times of Solomon, many farms had a barn. Most people were farmers back then. Barns were used for storage for crops and other grains to feed the farmer and their family, cattle, and other farm animals. Barns were a home for large farm animals such as cattle, pigs, and horses.

Red has been a traditional color of barns for two

Color the barn red and the silo brown

reasons. The first is the red color helps to hold in heat from the sun in the wintertime which keeps the inside of the barn warm. The second reason is the first substances ever used to protect the wood from damage on a barn consisted of linseed oil, (an orange-colored oil derived from the seeds of the flax plant), milk, lime, and iron oxide (or rust). Rust was found on old metal objects on farms and was a protector because it would kill any mold growing on the building. This combination acted as a long-lasting paint that would dry quickly. The rust caused the mixture to be *red* in color.

Verses to review:
Proverbs 3:9-10 Honor the Lord with your wealth, with the first fruits of all your crops: then your **barns** will be filled to overflowing.

When the barn is filled with cows, the farmer is blessed

Take Home Points:

It is important to be generous. Being generous means to 'have an attitude of giving', not taking! (Read **2 Corinthians 9:11**) First of all, we must understand anything that we have is a gift from God. All the money that we have comes from God. Our ability to make money comes from gifts he has given us, such as hard work. Sometimes we do not think that our ability to work hard is a gift, but it is! Other gifts we have are playing a musical instrument, being a carpenter, an engineer, a plumber, or an electrician. Rather than be selfish, let us honor God by giving back to him a portion of our gifts *first*. That means to take care of people around you who do not have as much as you. Make this a goal in your life. Maybe your barn is fuller with animals and crops for feeding your family than others. By helping others who are less fortunate than you, it shows love to others. Jesus said, "This is my commandment that you love one another, and your joy will be made full." (Read **John 15:11**) God will bless you more if you are generous. He can bless you with joy and peace, and in ways that you may not even know. If you have an allowance this week for doing chores around the house, learn to share some of it to those who do not have as much as you.

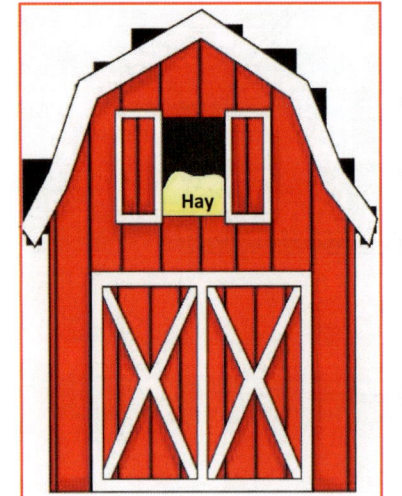

Other key verses:
2 Corinthians 9:11 Be generous on every occasion, and your generosity will result in thanksgiving to God.
John 15:11 Jesus said, "This is my commandment, that you love one another, and your joy will be made full."

Conclusion: Learn to be generous with all that you have, and God will be honored.

Clothing

Jesus with his disciples

Garments (outer clothing) worn in Bible times

Teachable Truths:

People in historic times wore garments or clothes made of animal skins to protect themselves or keep warm. Clothing later was made from natural fibers such as cotton, silk, and wool. Cotton and linen fabrics came from plants, wool was from sheep, and silk was produced by silkworms. People made different color clothes by dying them with berries or plants. Originally, pants did not have zippers or buttons. They simply used ties. Later, people wore clothing to protect themselves in battle

Knights wore heavy clothes and armor for protection

during wars. Knights in the Middle Ages (500 A.D. to 1492 A.D.) wore heavy clothing and helmets to protect themselves. Some clothing suggests a specific type of work, such as the uniforms that nurses, firefighters, and policemen wear. Doctors and lab technicians like to wear white coats. Clothes used to be made at home, but these days most are made in factories. In some countries, men wear skirts such as togas and kilts. While not common in most areas today, historically this style of dress was normal in places like Scotland.

Verse to review:
Proverbs 25:20 Like one who takes away a **garment** from a person on a cold day, or like vinegar poured on soda, is one who sings songs to a heavy heart.

Color the winter coat and scarves

Take Home Points:

For people living in Israel, wintertime temperatures can dip to freezing. It is even known to snow in Jerusalem! So warm clothing is necessary in that part of the world!

Only a nasty person would steal or take your coat on a cold day. Similarly, vinegar poured on soda causes a severe chemical reaction. Solomon says that this is the same thing as trying to help a hurting person (who has a heavy heart) by singing them songs.

HEAVY COATS are needed for a cold winter day

"Singing songs" is a figure of speech. It means taking "lightly" the discouragement that a friend is going through. If you want to give comfort to a hurting person, you do not want to be insensitive to their feelings. You do not want to be light and making jokes when someone is facing doom and gloom. We should help those who are hurting. That is what Jesus would do. (Read **Romans 12:15**)

Other key verses:
Romans 12:15 Rejoice with those who rejoice; mourn with those who mourn.

Conclusion: Help those who are in need. Be compassionate. Help those who are hurting.

Fire

Fire is important for heat and cooking

Teachable Truths:

Fire is a chemical reaction releasing heat and light. Fire has been used for thousands of years to help people cook food, keep homes warm during cold months, and to provide light. Substances (fuel) combine with oxygen in the air, not only producing a flame but also smoke. Fire requires fuel, oxygen, and heat to burn. Fuels include paper, wood, coal, or oil. Color tells us about the temperature of a candle flame. The inner part of the flame is light blue, with a temperature of around 1800 degree

Fire can be dangerous and burn wooden houses down quickly

Fahrenheit. That is the hottest part of the flame. The color becomes yellow, orange, and red on the outside of the flame. A fire will go out without fuel, oxygen, or heat. Fire is dangerous to humans as it can easily burn or blister skin. Fires in a house are controlled with a chimney, which exits from the roof. A chimney allows excess heat and smoke to escape the house.

Verse to review:
Proverbs 26:20 Without wood a fire goes out; without gossip an argument dies down.

Take Home Points:

Solomon shows how gossip and arguments can be similar. Gossip is talking about someone behind their back in a hurtful way. Arguments end quickly when people stop spreading rumors and wrong information about others.

Color the fire yellow and orange and the wood brown

Just like a fire goes out as soon as there is no more wood to burn. Along with gossip comes tattling, slander, and backbiting. Those who gossip love to stir up trouble rather than trying to bring peace. We should watch our lips and speech against saying anything negative about another. Also, do not talk so much. Cut your words in half if you must. The more you talk, the more likely you are to gossip. Learn to say nice things about people or do not say anything at all. (Read **Philippians 2:14**, **Colossians 4:6**)

Other key verses:
Philippians 2:14 Do everything without arguing or complaining.
Colossians 4:6 Let your conversation be always full of grace (kindness), seasoned with salt (good reasoning), so that you may know how to answer everyone.

Conclusion: Do everything without arguing or complaining. Stay away from gossip.

Lamp

A house oil lamp of Solomon's day

Teachable Truths:

Oil lamps were one of the most common household items of Bible times. They provided excellent light at night. Ceramic lamps like in the above picture were used all over the Mediterranean area from 2000 B.C. through the Middle Ages (500 A.D. to 1492 A.D.). They were used to burn oil- usually olive or sesame seed oil, fish oil, whale oil, or beeswax. The oil that was used depended on what was more abundant in the area. The lamp used a wick, made from fibers such as linen or papyrus that was put

Color the lamp gold

into the body of the lamp. The wick was lit, and a small flame came from the tip of the wick resting in a nozzle. The lamp could be set on any flat surface but was also could be carried in a person's hand. Lamps were also made from metals like bronze, stone, and alabaster. They were easier and safer to carry than torches, and they could be used over again.

Verse to review:
Proverbs 20:20 If a person curses his father or mother, his **lamp** will be snuffed out in pitch darkness.

Take Home Points:

Modern electric lamps provide light

This proverb teaches us that your life is affected by how you treat your parents. The household lamp, simple in its construction, provided the abundant light needed to walk in a dark place without falling. Imagine walking in the pitch-black darkness. We have all had to walk in the dark at times. We can end up stubbing our toes or even falling!

Solomon tells us in this proverb that our lives can end up having no direction if we *curse* (to bring harm or try to injure with speech) our parents. The lamp of a person is their spirit and soul. (Read **Proverbs 13:9**) Honoring your parents is key wisdom that God wants you to grasp and understand. You can live a longer life if you do so! (Read **Exodus 20:12, Ephesians 6:2-**

3) You can shorten your life by disrespecting your parents.

(Read **Deuteronomy 27:16**) The best way you can honor your parents is by obeying them when you are young, and then to take good care of them when they are old. This proverb brings Godly judgment on children who rebel against their parents.

Other Key Verses:
Proverbs 13:9 The light of the righteous shines brightly, but the lamp of the wicked is snuffed out.
Exodus 20:12 Honor your father and your mother, so that you may live long in the land of the Lord your God is giving you.
Ephesians 6:2-3 Honor your father and mother—which is the first commandment with a promise—that it may go well with you and that you may enjoy long life on the earth.
Deuteronomy 27:16 Cursed is the person who dishonors his father or his mother.

Conclusion: Treat your parents with honor and respect. Then your days on earth will be long.

Ornament(s)

Gold jewelry (ornaments) in Bible times

Teachable Truths:

Gold is considered a *valuable* metal all over the world. Having a gold necklace or gold earrings has been a sign of wealth. From the ancient Egyptians in 3000 B.C. to the modern U.S. Treasury, there are few metals that have had such a big role in human history. Gold was so important that the top stones on the Pyramids of Giza in Egypt were made from it. Most archaeological evidence shows people have always loved this shiny metal. Since gold is found all over the world, it has been mentioned numerous

KING SOLOMON was SO RICH that his goblets were made of GOLD!

times throughout ancient historical texts, including the Bible. When Solomon was King of Israel, it says this about gold in **1 Kings 10:21**: Nothing of value was made of silver- it had minimal value at that time. Everything of value was made of gold. **Genesis 2:10-12** describes the lands of Havilah, near the Garden of Eden, as a place where gold could be found. The Incans, Aztecs, and numerous other Indian civilizations in Mexico and Central America also used gold throughout their early history.

Verse to review:
Proverbs 25:12 Like an earring of gold or an **ornament** of fine gold is a wise person's rebuke (reprimand) to a listening ear.

Take Home Points:

In this proverb, Solomon is teaching two big pieces of wisdom! **#1**- it is important to be able to *accept criticism from an authority figure* or teacher and **#2**- it is important to *be a good listener* in your life. He is saying that these two principles are just like gold earrings, or a gold ornament necklace worn around your neck. Gold earrings are beautiful, and so are other ornaments made from this precious metal.

God puts forth his wisdom throughout the Bible. Learn his wisdom by reading and studying the Bible. In it, God instructs us on all important principles of life. God expects children to learn his wisdom from their parents and grandparents. (Read **Psalm 141:5**) What a fabulous opportunity. You need to be good listeners! If you get off the right path in life, expect your authority figures such as your parents, grandparents, and teachers to give you constructive criticism on how to fix things. (Read **1 Thessalonians 5:14**, **2 Timothy 2:24**) This should be done in a loving, instructional way. Then you can get back on the right path where you need to be.

God's wisdom taught in the Book of Proverbs is much more valuable than what you will ever learn at the university. Remember that!

Are you more valuable than pieces of gold in God's sight? Yes! What a wonderful warning with how we hear with good listening and speak. Do not be someone who rebels against these truths.

Other Key Verses:
1 Thessalonians 5:14 We urge you to warn those who are idle, encourage the timid, help the weak, be patient with everyone.
2 Timothy 2:24 And the Lord's servant must be kind to everyone, able to teach, not resentful.
Psalm 141:5 King David said, "Let a righteous person rebuke (reprimand) me—it is like oil on my head. It is kindness and I will not refuse it."

Conclusion: Learn to accept criticism well and be a good listener. Read and study the Bible.

Reaping and Sowing

Reap wheat at harvest with sowing of seed in springtime

Teachable Truths:

Many families living in Israel during the time of Solomon were farmers. They grew crops or took care of animals. Israelites learned the *science* of agriculture from the Egyptians. The *sowing* or planting seeds of various crops (especially wheat and barley) occurred during the spring months of March and April. Before seeds could be placed in the soil, the soil had to be prepared by plowing or "tilling". Simple plows were known in Israel during the time of Moses by 1500 B.C. The plows were

Using a sharp sickle to harvest wheat

light, and pulled by oxen, cows, or donkeys. The *reaping* of the grain at harvest-time in early fall of the year was performed either by pulling the crop up by the roots, or cutting it with a sickle. A sickle is a sharp knife-like object with a handle. The cut grain was generally put up in sheaves, and afterwards were gathered to be stored in barns. The time between *sowing* and *reaping* would be about four to five months.

Verse to review:
Proverbs 11:18 The wicked person earns deceptive pay, but the person who **sows** righteousness **reaps** a sure reward.

Take Home Points:
Children growing up during the time of Solomon would easily understand the principle of sowing and reaping. If their family sowed and planted seeds of

wheat in the springtime, they harvested wheat at harvest, not barley! If they sowed barley, they did not reap wheat! That makes perfect sense. If they did not keep the soil in their fields plowed or "tilled," they would end up with a lot of weeds choking their grains.

Color the ground, seeds, and plant

In this proverb, it is important for us to understand the meaning of wicked, deception, righteousness, and rewards. The wicked individual chases after the pleasures in a self-centered way. He or she cares nothing about the consequences of cheating to get what they want or in hurting others. Cheating can start early in our lives. Like cheating on a math test in second grade by looking at your neighbor's answers. This makes your test results better than they should be. People who live a life without God to direct them may get in trouble. They lie their way to success, which can lead to being guided by greed. The results of success are never satisfying because wicked people do not follow God. The temptation is that sin (living without God's principles in mind) can be fun, but it does not pay in the end!

Being righteous, on the other hand, will *give you a wonderful reward from God*. Being righteous means being good – and to give glory to God, not yourself. It means making the right decisions day by day. It means obeying your parents, teachers, and the law. It means living each day with the fruit of the Spirit. (Read **Galatians 5:22-23a**)

Make the RIGHT choices

When you are righteous, you may not see your reward for a while, because sowing follows reaping by many months. In fact, you may not see it until you get to heaven. The encouragement from this proverb is to never grow tired in doing what is right! (Read **Isaiah 40:29-31**, **Galatians 6:7,9**)

Other Key Verses:
Galatians 5:22-23a The fruit of the Spirit is love, joy, peace, patience, kindness, goodness, faithfulness, gentleness and self-control.
Isaiah 40:29-31 God gives strength to the tired and increase the power of the weak. Even children grow tired, and young people stumble and fall; but those who hope in the Lord will renew their strength. They will soar on wings like eagles; they will run and not grow tired; they will walk and not be faint.
Galatians 6:9 Let us not get tired of doing good, for at the proper time we will reap

a harvest if we do not give up.

> **Conclusion:** Work on being good and God will reward you for it. Do not give up!

Tent

A typical movable tent in Bible times

Teachable Truths:

Tents have been used for thousands of years for people to take a temporary shelter. They were popular in Solomon's day for families and people groups who would move around a lot from place to place. After the Israelites left Egypt in 1400 B.C., they traveled hundreds of miles. They entered Israel and lived in tents for 40 years before settling down in more permanent shelters. They were basically *nomads*. For a few million people, that is a lot of tents!

The main idea of a tent was that it was *portable*. Portable means the tent could be easily taken down and moved to a different location and "put up" again. Though moveable, a tent was generally able to protect the people living inside it from the outside weather such as a blistering sun, strong winds, or pelting rain. A tent acted as a home away from home and could give privacy and a nice place to sleep.

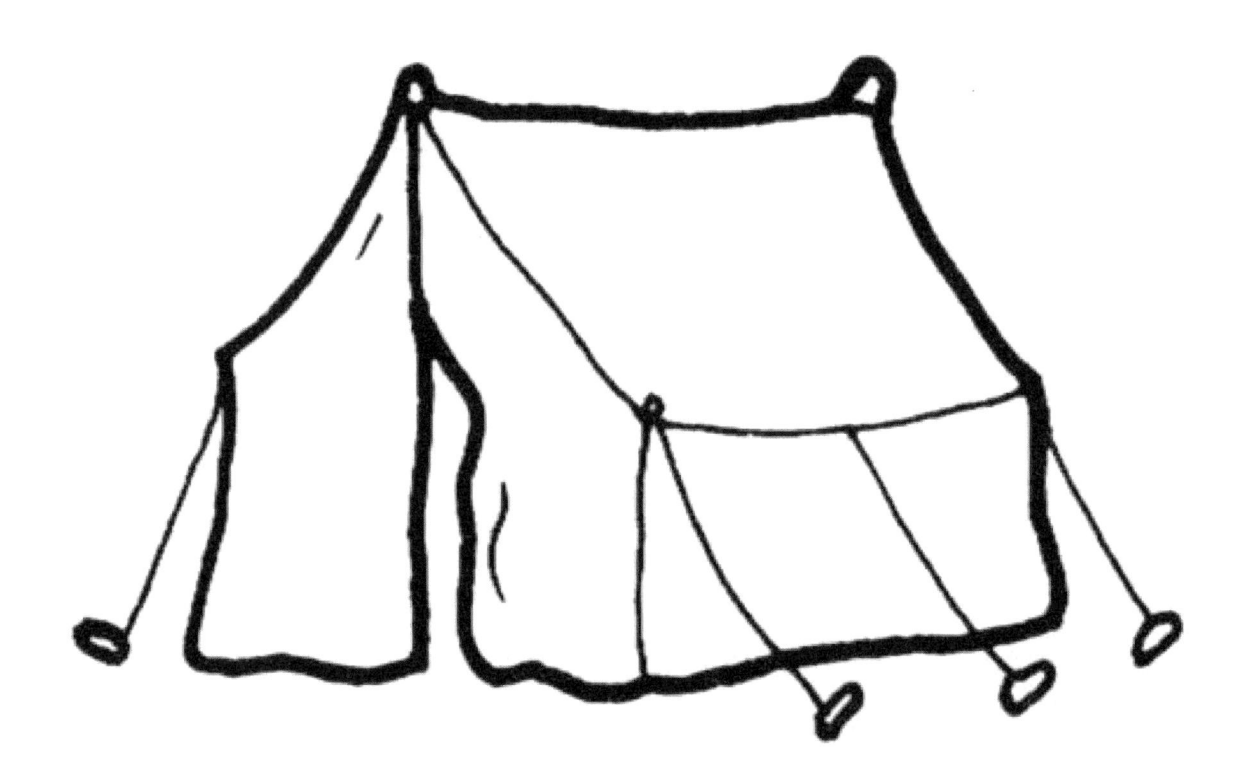

Color this camping tent green

Tents come in a variety of shapes and sizes. Many tents have useful features such as ventilation systems and weather-resistant covers. Many of these tents even include room dividers and doors!

Verse to review:
Proverbs 14:11 The house of the wicked will be destroyed, but the **tent** of the upright will flourish.

Take Home Points:

This proverb 'puts down' the wicked person and encourages the upright. God is telling us to pursue the right decisions in life that are good, think correctly, and try to have pure hearts. (Read **Philippians 4:8-9**)

What does the *wicked* mean? *The wicked do not think about God and they want to do their own thing.* They like to sin a lot! (Read **Psalm 10:4**) Houses are solid, permanent dwelling places for families. Unfortunately, the *wicked* who build their houses trust their wealth, smartness, and their physical strength more than

Even though this house in Bible times looks more secure than a tent, wicked people might live in it!

they trust God. These houses look good on the outside, but inside the house there are major problems with the people living there. The upright may **only** have a temporary, portable tent to live in, which on the outside, does not compare to the solid house in appearance. But God blesses the people living in the tent because they try to be righteous.

In this proverb, there can be a temptation for the person living in the tent to be jealous of the person living in a house, because they may have more money. But God tells us not to be jealous about our neighbor's house, but to be satisfied with what we have. (Read the 10th commandment in **Exodus 20:17a**) An important story teaches this principle is in the New Testament in **Luke 16:19-31**. The beggar Lazarus was poor, covered with sores, and had no house, but he was full of joy in heaven, his permanent dwelling place. He had happiness there, but not on earth. On the other hand, the rich man lived in a luxurious mansion in his earthly life, but for eternity had pain in hell, separated from God. His earthly wealth was destroyed by God.

Examples	The Wicked	The Righteous
Loves God		★
Likes to bully others	★	
Will cheat to get ahead	★	
Takes care of the poor		★
Honors their parents		★
Is selfish	★	
Gossips about others	★	
Lies a lot	★	
Helps the less fortunate		★

Other Key Verses:
Philippians 4:8-9 Whatever is true, whatever is noble, whatever is right, whatever is pure, whatever is lovely, whatever is admirable—if anything is excellent or praiseworthy—think about such things. Whatever you have learned, put into practice.
Psalm 10:4 In their pride the wicked does not seek him; in all their thoughts there is no room for God.
Exodus 20:17a You shall not covet (strongly desire) your neighbor's house.

Conclusion: God says your heart is more important than what kind of house that you live in.

Well

A village well for obtaining fresh water in Bible times

Teachable Truths:

Wells have been dug for centuries to provide fresh water for drinking and bathing when a river or lake was not nearby. A well may be 30 feet deep or more. Throughout history, most cities that were not close to fresh water lakes or rivers got their water from wells.

The water that is trapped below the ground in spaces above rock is called *groundwater,* and this is the water used for water wells. The world's oceans

Color the well gray, and the roof and the pail brown

contain around 97% of all the water, but it is not drinkable because it is too salty. Around 2% is frozen in glaciers at the North and South poles. Out of the 1% left over, *groundwater* makes up about 96%. The rest is in streams, lakes, and rivers. Polluted groundwater can cause illnesses that affect the stomach and other parts of the body. About 25% of the water that falls in the U.S annually becomes groundwater. Wells typically never run dry and can last at least 30 years.

Verse to review:
Proverbs 25:26 Like a muddied spring or a polluted **well** is a righteous person who gives way to the wicked.

Take Home Points:

Wells were important in Israel at the time of Solomon and found in many villages. This was true in areas where it did not rain much. Nothing worse than a well that did not consistently give water or one that gave water that was not pure.

This modern day well in Africa gives PURE water to the villagers

This proverb tells us to be salt and light while living on the earth as well as not to compromise on your godly lifestyle and principles. (Read **Matthew 5:13**,14) The Christian must resist the temptation to live like the rest of the world who have forgotten about God. Righteous people are to be wells of pure water to those around them. They are to live guided by the principles set forth in the Bible. Remember that wicked people do not put God first in their lives. They put their own desires ahead of God. You must live and work in the world. But many people in the world love to mock the Bible and Christians. It is your duty to be like pure water from a well. (Read **1 Timothy 1:5**) You must resist the wickedness of the world. Resist being a hypocrite. A hypocrite says that they are a Christian, but they do not act like it; they act like the rest of the

Jesus said to the children, "If you know me, you know God."

world who do not have a personal relationship with God. (Read **1 Peter 2:1**)

Other Key Verses:
Matthew 5:13-14 You are the salt of the earth. But if the salt loses its saltiness, how can it be made salty again? You are the light of the world. A city on a hill cannot be hidden.
1 Timothy 1:5 Love comes from a pure heart and a good conscience and a sincere faith.
1 Peter 2:1 Rid yourselves of all evil and all lying, hypocrisy, envy, and slander of every kind.

> **Conclusion:** Learn to have a pure heart, and live like a person who has godly values.

Following God

Do you want to follow God?

Through Jesus and the Holy Spirit, God will change your life! You will then make God first in your life and make him Lord of all your decisions. Parents and grandparents, you can walk your children and grandchildren through these steps below. **John 3:16** says "This is how much God loved the world: He gave his Son, his one and only Son. Why? So that no one need be destroyed; by believing in him, anyone can have a whole and everlasting life." This is a key verse in the Bible. The apostle Paul shared the Gospel, or the Good News for all humans, to us in the New Testament **1 Corinthians 15:3-7**. "The first thing I did was place before you what was placed so emphatically before me: that the Messiah died for our sins, exactly as Scripture tells it; that he was buried; that he was raised from death on the third day, again exactly as Scripture says; that he presented himself alive to Peter, then to his closest followers, and later to more than five hundred of his followers all at the same time, most of them still around (although a few have since died); that he then spent time with James and the rest of those he commissioned to represent him; and that he finally presented himself alive to me."

The following steps are found in the New Testament Book of Romans:

Step #1- We must all realize that we are sinners and that we need forgiveness. We are not worthy of God's grace. Right now, admit that you are a sinner, and need God. **Romans 3:23** "For all have sinned and fall short of the glory of God." That is, nobody deserves to go to heaven to be with Jesus on their own merit.

Step #2- Through Jesus, God gave us a way to be saved from our sins. God showed us his love by giving us the potential for life through the death of his Son, Jesus Christ. Do you believe this with all your heart? **Romans 5:8** "But God demonstrates his love toward us, in that, while we were still sinners, Christ died for us." An incredible act of grace and mercy.

Step #3- If we remain in sin, we will die and not go to heaven. However, if we accept Jesus as our Lord and Savior, and repent of our sins, we will have eternal life. **Romans 6:23** "For the deserved punishment of sin is death, but the free gift of God is eternal life in Christ Jesus our Lord."

Step #4- Romans 10:9 "If you confess with your mouth the Lord Jesus and believe in your heart that God has raised Him from the dead (the resurrection), you will be saved and go to heaven *and* be saved from hell."

"Saved" means going to heaven forever. You can never be saved by trying to be a good person, nor can you be saved through any amount of 'doing good'. **Ephesians 2:8-9** says "For by grace have you been saved by faith. And that, not of yourselves. It is the gift of God, not of works. Lest any person should boast.

Proverbs in this Book

Proverbs 3:9-10 Honor the Lord with your wealth, with the first fruits of all your crops: then your **barns** will be filled to overflowing.

Proverbs 11:18 The wicked person earns deceptive pay, but the person who **sows** righteousness **reaps** a sure reward.

Proverbs 14:11 The house of the wicked will be destroyed, but the **tent** of the upright will flourish.

Proverbs 20:20 If a person curses his father or mother, his **lamp** will be snuffed out in pitch darkness.

Proverbs 25:12 Like an earring of gold or an **ornament** of fine gold is a wise person's rebuke (reprimand) to a listening ear.

Proverbs 25:20 Like one who takes away a **garment** (clothing) from a person on a cold day, or like vinegar poured on soda, is one who sings songs to a heavy heart.

Proverbs 25:26 Like a muddied spring or a polluted **well** is a righteous person who gives way to the wicked.

Proverbs 26:20 Without wood a **fire** goes out; without gossip an argument dies down.

Principles Taught in this Book

- Be generous
- Be a good listener
- Take care of the less fortunate
- Do not be a complainer
- Respect your parents
- Accept criticism well
- Do not be jealous
- Your heart is more important than your house
- Think about good things
- Live right

Printed in Dunstable, United Kingdom